A Touch of the Tiny Hacketts

First seen on BBC-TV in the 1978–79 Play for Today season, *A Touch of the Tiny Hacketts* is a comedy of modern suburban life by John Esmonde and Bob Larbey, creators of *The Good Life*. Ray and Sylvia are in bed in their bungalow when they hear an intruder. Grabbing his Zulu knobkerrie – an unwanted present from friends they haven't seen for years – Ray lays the burglar out cold. But when the intruder turns out to be what Ray's boss, would call an Unfortunate, Ray's 'heroic' ironic consequences . . .

Play for Today
Published in association with BBC-TV of *all* the autumn '78 Plays for Today. simultaneously with first transmission. overleaf.

The cover photograph shows Ray Brooks as Ray and Brenda Bruce as Mrs Hackett in the BBC-TV production of A Touch of the Tiny Hacketts, *produced and directed by James Cellan-Jones.*
BBC Copyright photograph by Iain Coates.

The **Play for Today** series

Nina *by Jehane Markham*
Victims of Apartheid *by Tom Clarke*
A Touch of the Tiny Hacketts *by John Esmonde and Bob Larbey*
Dinner at the Sporting Club *by Leon Griffiths*
Donal and Sally *by James Duthie*
Audience & Private View *by Vaclav Havel*
Soldiers Talking Cleanly *by Mike Stott*
One Bummer Newsday *by Andy McSmith*

John Esmonde and Bob Larbey

A Touch of the Tiny Hacketts

EYRE METHUEN · LONDON
in association with BBC-TV

First published in 1978 by Eyre Methuen Ltd
11 New Fetter Lane, London EC4P 4EE

Filmset by Northumberland Press Ltd,
Gateshead, Tyne & Wear
Printed in Great Britain by Richard Clay (The Chaucer Press) Ltd,
Bungay, Suffolk

ISBN 0 413 45600 5

A TOUCH OF THE TINY HACKETTS was first presented by BBC Television on 31 October 1978, with the following cast:

RAYMOND COLLIS	Ray Brooks
SYLVIA COLLIS	Judy Cornwell
TINY HACKETT	Rusty Goffe
FIRST POLICEMAN	Karl Howman
SECOND POLICEMAN	Hugh Walters
NORMAN TUCK	Nat Jackley
FIRST AMBULANCE MAN	Tim Meats
STAN	Tony Selby
C.I.D. MAN	Alec Linstead
TERRY	Douglas Fisher
OLD SPUD	George Tovey
GRAHAM	George Innes
MIKE	Anthony Langdon
MISS BENSON	Deborah Fairfax
REPORTER	Eamonn Boyce
MR NESBITT	Patrick Newell
MR SAMSON	John Kidd
COURT ATTENDANT/USHER	Esmond Webb
MRS HACKETT	Brenda Bruce

Produced and directed by James Cellan-Jones
Designed by Ray Cusick

1. Exterior. London suburban road. Night.

Longshot of bungalow – no lights. Dim torch light flashes in front room. Pause.

2. Interior. Bedroom. Night.

Raymond and Sylvia Collis are asleep. Raymond is in his middle forties – Sylvia a little younger. We hear the distant sound of a jug being smashed. This wakes Sylvia instantly. She listens but hears nothing more and is about to dismiss it and go back to sleep when she hears a door creak. She sits up and listens intently. Further indistinguishable but definite noises confirm her suspicions.

SYLVIA. It is. (*She shakes her husband.*) Raymond! There's somebody in the house!

She has whispered this and Raymond does not wake up fully.

RAYMOND. No.

SYLVIA (*still whispering*). There is. Go and look. There's somebody in in the house!

She half-pushes Raymond out of bed. He makes the rest of the move alone and stumbles sleepily towards the bedroom door like a million husbands who have been sent to investigate imaginary noises in the night.

RAYMOND. It never is anybody.

3. Interior. Hall. Night.

We see from the geography that the Collises live in a small bungalow. As part of the decoration of the hall, a Zulu knobkerrie hangs on the wall on two hooks. Raymond comes out of the bedroom and starts along the hall, still half asleep. He does not turn the light on. The door to the sitting room suddenly opens and Raymond nearly collides with what looks like a crouching figure. Raymond shouts in fear and shock. He snatches the knobkerrie from the wall and strikes out – a reflex action. There is a groan and the figure falls to the floor. Sylvia comes out of the bedroom.

SYLVIA. Raymond! What's going on?

She switches on the hall light. Raymond turns to her.

RAYMOND. I hit him. He came out of the front room. I hit him.

Sylvia is staring past Raymond. Raymond turns. The man Raymond hit lies unconscious. He is a dwarf. A zip holdall is on the floor beside him. Raymond stares, unbelieving.

Oh! He's only . . . he's a dwarf.

SYLVIA (*of the knobkerrie*). And you hit him with that?

RAYMOND. I didn't know.

SYLVIA. You never bloody well do, do you?

4. Exterior. Street. Night.

A street of non-posh bungalows in an outer London area – the sort of district that provides the man-power for faceless light industries. A police car and an ambulance are drawn up outside Raymond and Sylvia's home. One policeman is in the car, using the radio. The door of the bungalow is open. Up the road one of two lights have been turned on and the odd light-sleepers have turned out to have a nose, but the only close spectator is Norman Tuck, a pensioner and his old mongrel dog. The policeman gets out of the car and goes back towards the house.

TUCK. Police eh?

There is no answer to this as is shown by the expression on the policeman's face. He goes into the house.

5. Interior. Hall. Night.

Two ambulance men are kneeling over the dwarf. Raymond and Sylvia, now wearing dressing gowns, look on. Raymond is trembling with post-action shock. He searches for Sylvia's hand but she moves ever so slightly away. Raymond looks over the dwarf to a second policeman (a young one) for some reassurance. But the policeman holds the knobkerrie. He looks from it to the dwarf, to Raymond. His look is so carefully neutral that it implies disapproval. Raymond smiles nervously and gets nothing back at all. The awkward silence is broken by the entry of the first policeman from the car.

FIRST POLICEMAN (*to ambulance men*). What's the form lads?

FIRST AMBULANCE MAN. Hospital.

The ambulance men go out.

SYLVIA (*to Raymond*). They'll want a statement.

RAYMOND. Oh. Yes. (*To policemen.*) Shall I give you my statement?

FIRST POLICEMAN. First things first sir, if you don't mind.

This makes Raymond horribly aware of the dwarf again.

SECOND POLICEMAN. Seen this?

He hands the knobkerrie to the first policeman who repeats the look from it to Raymond to the dwarf.

RAYMOND. It's a knobkerrie. Zulus use them.

SECOND POLICEMAN. *Do* they?

The ambulance men come back with a stretcher. They manoeuvre the dwarf (Tiny Hackett) onto the stretcher, being particularly gentle with his head, which they support with a small sandbag on either side. They cover him with a blanket.

FIRST AMBULANCE MAN. And – up! (*They lift the stretcher.*) (*To policemen.*) St James's.

FIRST POLICEMAN. Right-ho mate. There'll be somebody along later. (*The ambulance men carry Tiny out.*) Now then . . .

RAYMOND. I didn't know he was a dwarf when I hit him. I mean, I wouldn't hit a dwarf to save my life.

SYLVIA (*to policemen*). Perhaps you'd like to come through.

She indicates the sitting room and they go in. Sylvia stops Raymond following.

Now listen. When you make a statement, you have to weigh your words. That's what a statement is – it's a statement, not a confession.

6. Exterior. Street. Night.

Norman Tuck is still hanging about with his dog Prince as the ambulance men come down the path carrying the stretcher. Tuck hurries to open the gate.

TUCK. You'd be taking him to hospital then would you?

FIRST AMBULANCE MAN. It seems the right thing to do, yes.

TUCK. Oh yes. Definitely. Of course, they all go to St James's from round here you know.

FIRST AMBULANCE MAN. That's right.

Tuck follows them and watches as they load the stretcher into the ambulance. The size of the patient registers for the first time.

TUCK. Now there's a thing. He doesn't come down to the end of that stretcher. (*Almost accusingly.*) You haven't got a normal-sized person there.

FIRST AMBULANCE MAN. Oh push off, you nosey old sod!

TUCK. Oh nice. Very nice. Call yourselves Ambulance Men? You're not even civil.

They ignore him, get into the cab and drive off..

TUCK (*to Prince*). That was a dwarf Prince and they're not telling me anything different.

7. Interior. Kitchen. Night.

One window is open, with one of its panes of glass broken. The broken glass is on the draining board. Raymond, Sylvia and the first policeman are seated at the kitchen table, the policeman with a notebook. The second policeman is looking at the broken window. On the table is Tiny's holdall – in front of it are various items which he had obviously put in the bag. The knobkerrie is on the table as well.

SYLVIA. Wouldn't we be more comfortable in the other room? Raymond could light the fire.

FIRST POLICEMAN. No, this is fine. (*Wanting to get rid of her.*) Look, if you'd like to get dressed . . .

SYLVIA. No. I'll stay.

FIRST POLICEMAN. Right then. (*To Raymond.*) Where were we? Oh yes. And you then struck the intruder with the club.

RAYMOND. Yes.

SYLVIA. No, not club. I don't think you should put 'club'. It sounds as though you're clubbing somebody. Put knobkerrie.

FIRST POLICEMAN. Very well madam – 'knobkerrie'.

SECOND POLICEMAN. The Zulus use them.

The first policeman allows himself a little smile.

RAYMOND. I didn't buy it. I mean, it's not the sort of thing I'd go out and purchase. It was a present you see.

SECOND POLICEMAN. From a Zulu?

FIRST POLICEMAN (*warning*). Chas!

RAYMOND. I mean, we haven't seen them for ages but we still exchange Christmas presents and this just arrived.

FIRST POLICEMAN (*not interested*). I see, yes.

RAYMOND. They live in Durban. I've got their address. I mean if you want to write to them to verify that they will back me up that it was only sent as a curio.

The second policeman's walkie-talkie crackles and emits an indistinguishable question. He leans towards the window for better reception.

SECOND POLICEMAN. Yes all right. Tell them to put it on top of the first-aid cabinet.

RAYMOND. Pardon?

The second policeman just points to his walkie-talkie.

Oh. (*To first policeman.*) O.K? Yes. I'll get that for you now if you like.

FIRST POLICEMAN. What?

RAYMOND. Their address.

FIRST POLICEMAN. We're not really interested in that sir.

SYLVIA. Just stick to the point Raymond. (*Pointing to the policeman's notes.*) Go on from 'Knobkerrie' – it's. I.E. incidentally. Go on from there.

FIRST POLICEMAN. Right. Now then Mr Collis. Did you pick up the . . . weapon before you left the bedroom?

RAYMOND. Yes.

SYLVIA. No. He didn't.

RAYMOND. That's right. I didn't.

SYLVIA. Look, should we have a solicitor here?

FIRST POLICEMAN. All we're trying to do is get the facts down.

SYLVIA (*to Raymond*). Well get them right then.

RAYMOND. I'm sorry. I'm just a bit out of gear. I've never had dealings with the Police before.

SYLVIA. No, he hasn't. Put that down.

The first policeman sighs and writes.

FIRST POLICEMAN. 'Mr Collis has never had dealings with the Police before.'

SYLVIA. Right.

FIRST POLICEMAN. Well Mr Collis?

The second policeman's walkie-talkie crackles again.

SECOND POLICEMAN. Well put some greaseproof paper under it!

RAYMOND. Yes, that's right. We keep it in the hall – on two hooks – you can see them out there . . . and I saw what I thought was a crouching figure and I grabbed it and just lashed out.

SECOND POLICEMAN (*just loud enough to be heard*). Huh.

SYLVIA. In the dark – put 'In the dark.'

RAYMOND. Then Sylvia turned the light on and we saw him and I felt . . . well, I don't know what I felt.

SYLVIA. Which is why it was me who telephoned you and the Ambulance people. I haven't touched anything, incidentally.

FIRST POLICEMAN. Very wise madam, because the C.I.D. will want to have a look round tomorrow.

SECOND POLICEMAN. It certainly won't be tonight – not with him.

FIRST POLICEMAN. Oh give it a rest Chas. He put his thing through beforehand.

SECOND POLICEMAN. All right, I've said my piece.

The first policeman realises that Raymond and Sylvia do not know what they are talking about.

FIRST POLICEMAN. Yes, in the morning I should think. Well, I think that's all I need.

RAYMOND. Thank you.

SYLVIA. So what happens now then? What's the next step?

FIRST POLICEMAN. Oh I see. Well all the reports get what we call collated and then forwarded on to the C.I.D. who then review these reports and decide whether or not they get forwarded on again to the D.P.P.

SYLVIA. What's that.

FIRST POLICEMAN. Director of Public Prosecutions – who, in turn, decides whether or not there is, in fact, a case to answer.

Raymond and Sylvia are surprised.

RAYMOND. Well there must be a case to answer! You've got the bloke – the window's broken – he had some of our things in his bag.

SYLVIA. Yes. What more do you want?

FIRST POLICEMAN. Oh I wasn't referring to the burglary side of the matter. That's all clear cut. I was referring to whether or not your husband has a case to answer.

This is a shock.

RAYMOND. Me? What have I done?

SECOND POLICEMAN. Well it would come under the heading of Grievous Bodily Harm or possibly Attempted Murder.

This sounds awful.

RAYMOND. But they wouldn't would they? It's a man's house. I didn't ask him to burgle me ... and ... would they?

SYLVIA. Because if you're saying that you've just twisted everything we've said.

The first policeman gets up. He has had enough of Sylvia.

FIRST POLICEMAN. You don't understand the system madam. There are departments involved here. Anyway, you'll be kept informed. It's not my decision. Chas.

They make to go.

RAYMOND. But it was self-defence.

SECOND POLICEMAN. You're saying he actually attacked you now are you?

RAYMOND. No, but he could have done. I didn't know what he was going to do.

SECOND POLICEMAN. Look, if it comes to anything, that will be decided in the Magistrates Court.

RAYMOND. But that's not right.

SECOND POLICEMAN (*his hostility beginning to show*). Well you should have thought of that ... (*His walkie-talkie crackles again.*) What? Well wipe it off! It's washable.

FIRST POLICEMAN. Come on Chas. Goodnight then. We'll see ourselves out.

They go. Raymond sits stunned.

8. Exterior. Street. Night.

The policemen come out of the bungalow and down the path towards their car. The other nosey parkers have given up and gone back to bed but Norman Tuck is still hanging about with Prince.

TUCK. Here they come – the boys in blue!

The first policeman recognises him.

FIRST POLICEMAN. Are you still here?

TUCK. I'm taking Prince for a walk. So what's been going on then? What's the strength of it?

FIRST POLICEMAN. Nothing to do with you Pop – just a break-in. Off you go.

TUCK (*not moving*). If you want to hold me over as a witness, I'm only too willing you know.

FIRST POLICEMAN. I don't think that will be necessary.

TUCK. Only if you do, I live just round the corner – next to Bantocks the pet food people – very handy for Prince of course, and you can take my statement any night of the week – except for Wednesdays of course.

FIRST POLICEMAN. Enjoy your walk.

TUCK. Because they tell you don't they? There's advertisements about it – I've seen them. 'Have a go' they say – 'Back up your Police Force.' That is what I am doing – offering myself as a witness.

SECOND POLICEMAN. All right, what did you actually witness?

TUCK. Quite a lot of things for your information.

SECOND POLICEMAN. What?

TUCK. I saw you come. I saw the ambulance come. I saw the ambulance people go – and now I've witnessed you come out of the house looking serious.

SECOND POLICEMAN. Have you got a licence for that dog?

TUCK. Yes I have, and I've got the whole of Battersea Dogs Home to back me up to that effect!

FIRST POLICEMAN. Come on Chas, it'll be stone cold. Thanks all the same Pop.

They get into their car but Tuck still talks to them through the window.

TUCK. That little bloke they brought out doesn't live there you know. The Collises live there. (*The second policeman winds up the window.*) I can put two and two together just as well as you can! (*The car drives off.*) Come on Prince. (*He hurries to the corner of the street where there is a telephone box. They go on.*) In you come Prince. Nice and warm in here. Now, where is it? (*He takes out his wallet and finds a number on a piece of paper. He looks at it and dials.*) It's ringing Prince. Ah! (*He presses in his coin.*) Hello? Night desk please. Hello? My name is Norman Tuck, 37 Rothnall Road, Hounslow – you have used one or two of my little scoops before. Yes. Well this is a big one. There has been a break-in at number 11 Maycroft Close at the home of a Mr and Mrs Collis – I think the initial is R but your boys can check on that. No, that is not all! (*To Prince.*) Rush, rush, rush – they don't give you a chance do they? (*To phone.*) After the incident a dwarf was seen – by me – to be carried – unconscious – on a stretcher – from the house. Yes, I'm positive. Well St James's I suppose. They all go to St James's from round here. Well unless there were two burglars I would have assumed that he was, wouldn't you? Yes, well that's for you to check isn't it? Oy, before you go. I want my name to remain anonymous in this matter and I expect you to honour your usual practice of making an ex gratia payment should an article be published deriving out of my information. Right. Thank you very much. Goodbye then. Have you gone? Oh. Goodbye then. (*He hangs up and puts his wallet away.*) Alert ears, alert eyes and make yourself a few bob eh Prince? Here, look at the top of your head. You aren't half going grey.

They leave the phone box.

9. Interior. Hall. Day.

Raised voices from the kitchen – Raymond and Sylvia's. The door chimes go. Raymond comes out of the kitchen to answer.

RAYMOND. I *am* your husband!

He opens the front door. The caller is Stan – about the same age as Raymond but with all the confidence that Raymond lacks – confidence born out of an ability to make telling the time sound important.

Hello Stan.

Stan comes straight in.

10. Interior. Kitchen. Day.

STAN (*almost accusingly*). Why didn't you tell me? Good God, I'm only five minutes away. All you had to do was lift up the telephone and I would have been round.

Stan goes straight through to the kitchen. Sylvia is already pouring Stan a cup of tea. She hands it to him as he comes in.

STAN. Why didn't you tell me Sylvia?

SYLVIA. Oh it was awful Stan – the most awful night of my life.

STAN. Of course it was. I'm just sorry that you didn't call me that's all.

Raymond has followed Stan in.

RAYMOND. We would have Stan, but everything just happened on top of each other, you know.

STAN. I do know Ray, but that's all the more reason for bringing a clear head to bear, instead of which, what do I get? Mrs Ammonds jumping out in the road as I came round the corner in the car.

SYLVIA (*worried*). What does she know then?

STAN. I'm not giving her version houseroom Sylvia because it's bound to be garbled.

SYLVIA. Well what did she say?

STAN. Well she reckoned you were broken into last night.

SYLVIA. Yes?

She sits down.

STAN. By a gang of people from the Leeward Islands. Now I'm not taking that into credence. She said that one of them fell off your roof. Nobody did fall off your roof did they?

RAYMOND. No, of course they didn't.

STAN. That's what I told her. Well what actually did happen then?

There is a pause.

RAYMOND (*carefully*). We did have a break-in Stan, but we don't really want to talk about it.

STAN. Oh. O.K. Fine. I pride myself on being a respecter of persons and their privacies and you know, about all, that I love you two people very much, you know that don't you?

RAYMOND. Thanks Stan.

Stan now waits to be told. He isn't.

STAN. I'll only say this. If I don't know the facts I don't see how I can help you.

RAYMOND. To do what?

STAN. There will be ramifications Ray – there always are – and, without blowing my own trumpet, I am the one aren't I – to guide you through them?

RAYMOND. There will be ramifications, agreed.

STAN. Well there you are then. Only I'm fighting for you with my hands tied behind my back. I'm fighting for you in the dark. I mean, if I'd been in the dark with your crazy paving, where would the house improvement grant have come from? Fortunately I knew all the facts and was able to put Mr Ridley on to your crazy paving within two hours.

Sylvia has been thinking.

SYLVIA. I think you ought to know what happened Stan. It's bound to be talked about and people do listen to you.

STAN. Only because I have lived in the world Sylvia.

SYLVIA. Ray.

RAYMOND. Yes, all right. Well we did have a burglar. Sylvie woke me up. I came out and virtually bumped into him in the dark. So I snatched up that knobkerrie thing and hit him.

STAN (*surprised*). You?

RAYMOND. Yes. Then Sylvia turned the light on and . . .

Sylvia gets in quickly.

SYLVIA. And there he was on the floor – out cold with our ornaments.

STAN. Blimey.

SYLVIA. So, of course, I phoned the ambulance and police and what not and they took him off to hospital.

RAYMOND. He was still unconscious.

STAN. I see. (*They wait as if for Stan to deliver his verdict. Suddenly he gets up and raises Raymond's arm aloft*). Then three cheers for Raymond Collis is what I say.

RAYMOND. No, don't Stan. I don't feel good about it.

STAN. Then you damn well should. You have struck a blow for the Englishman and his castle. I'll be frank with you Ray. I didn't think you had it in you, but it's about time somebody stuck up for us mortgage-owners. Put him in hospital eh?

RAYMOND. Yes.

STAN. Well for a man who's done what a lot of other people just talk about you're not looking very cock-a-hoop.

RAYMOND. I don't feel it.

STAN. Why? There's nothing you haven't told me is there?

RAYMOND. No. Nothing.

STAN. Well then. Huh! So much for my ramifications. Open and shut case as they say.

RAYMOND. That's the thing . . .

STAN. What?

Sylvia gets up.

SYLVIA. Here, look at the time. You're going to be late for work Stan.

STAN. You're right. Come on Ray. It looks as though I'm going to have to walk in your shadow all day long, eh?

RAYMOND. No, I'm not going in this morning. We've got the C.I.D. coming.

STAN. Oh yes, that is correct. They do come. Look, if you want me to stay . . .

SYLVIA. No, it's very good of you Stan but I think we'll be all right.

STAN. Oh I'm sure you will be. (*Laughing.*) I'm sure the new Raymond can cope with anything that comes along now. (*Raymond smiles weakly. Stan gets up.*) Only I'll just say this. If a ramification of any sort should turn up, don't exclude old Stan this time eh? (*To Ray.*) See you this afternoon – champ!

He claps Raymond on the shoulder and goes out. Sylvia goes with him. Raymond slumps at the table, wishing that it was yesterday and all this had never happened. He becomes aware that he has put his elbow in the upturned foil top of the milk bottle on the table. He irritably brushes cream from his sleeve. Sylvia comes back into the kitchen.

RAYMOND. I wish we could have a milk jug on the breakfast table just for once!

She sees straight through this.

SYLVIA. Don't get petulant Raymond, just because you can't have your own way.

RAYMOND. It's ridiculous. I'm the one who's been burgled. I shouldn't have to cover anything up.

SYLVIA. It's not as simple as that and you know it. You haven't put a man in hospital. You've put a dwarf in hospital.

RAYMOND. Dwarves are men.

SYLVIA. Not in the public's eye they're not. Which is why we stick to what we told Stan. We had a burglar, just a burglar. You hit him and he's in hospital.

RAYMOND. It can't be that simple. It'll get out.

SYLVIA. How?

RAYMOND. It will.

SYLVIA. How?

RAYMOND. Things do.

SYLVIA. All right, apart from us, who knows about it? The Police and the Ambulance people, and who are they? Do we know them? Do they know us? Do they know any people round here? And anyway, they're not supposed to talk about anything – they're duty bound, I'm sure they are.

RAYMOND. And what if I get charged with Attempted Murder? What if I have to go to Court?

SYLVIA. I'll cross that bridge when I come to it – if I come to it.

RAYMOND. And in the meantime, I've got to go round lying.

SYLVIA. It's not lying. It's just not saying too much.

RAYMOND. But why should I have to? Why should I have to?

SYLVIA. I don't understand you. What do you want to do? Stand on the Town Hall balcony with a megaphone and shout to all and sundry that you could be an attempted murderer and that your victim was a dwarf?

RAYMOND. No.

SYLVIA. Well then?

RAYMOND. What?

SYLVIA. What *do* you want?

RAYMOND. I don't know. I've just got a feeling that I shouldn't be on the receiving end of it all.

SYLVIA. You should have thought of that last night.

RAYMOND. I didn't have time to think.

SYLVIA. Well you've got time now, so think! If this all blows over, you might come out of it quite well – people might even have a bit of respect for you which is not anything you're exactly famous for is it?

The door chimes go.

SYLVIA. It's you I'm thinking of Raymond.

11. Front door. Day.

Sylvia goes to answer the door.

C.I.D. Good morning. Mrs Collis?

SYLVIA. Yes.

C.I.D. C.I.D.

SYLVIA. Oh yes. Come in. (*Calling.*) Raymond! It's the people from the (*lowering her voice*) C.I.D.

12. Exterior. Bungalow. Day.

Sylvia comes out and looks up and down the road for any nosey neighbour. There is one, who stands on her doorstep being obviously nosey.

SYLVIA. For goodness' sake go in Mrs Ammonds. You're like a bloody fixture on that doorstep.

Sylvia goes in and closes the door.

13. Interior. Living room. Day.

The C.I.D. man is dusting for fingerprints around the window. He whistles through his teeth as he works. Raymond and Sylvia hover behind him. Sylvia nudges Raymond.

SYLVIA (*mouthing*). Go on. Ask him.

RAYMOND. Um ... How's it going?

C.I.D. Coming along.

RAYMOND. Good. (*Slaps his thigh.*)

SYLVIA (*mouthing*). *Ask* him!

RAYMOND. I wondered if there was any news – if you're allowed to tell me what that is – I mean, any news about me being charged with anything.

C.I.D. It hasn't gone up yet. My report has to go with it.

SYLVIA. Well when will we know?

C.I.D. Shouldn't take long. He should have it all on his desk this morning.

Raymond's frustration comes to the surface.

RAYMOND. In the meantime I've got to wait and sweat and worry whether or not I'm going to be charged with Attempted Murder. It seems unbelievable. It seems that if you catch a burglar what you should say is, 'Here you are mate. I've put all my valuables in a bag for you. Perhaps you'd like a cup of tea or something before you go because I'm not going to touch you in case *I* get charged with something!' It's not right.

C.I.D. You have got it out of proportion haven't you? You're not being singled out you know. This is absolutely standard procedure if there's any injury to any burglar in any house. More often than not the D.I. looks at the facts and says, 'No. There's nothing to answer there' and tosses it out.

RAYMOND (*relieved*). Oh. So it's only more or less a formality?

C.I.D. More often than not. Unless there are any special circumstances.

SYLVIA. Like what?

C.I.D. Well – it depends – say the burglar died.

RAYMOND. How is he?

C.I.D. What, your particular one? Wait a minute, I did hear something when I came on this morning. Yes – last I heard they thought his skull might be fractured.

Close up of Raymond. He is terrified.

14. Exterior. Works. Day.

A small light industry establishment – pretty old-fashioned. Raymond walks in through the gates and past what is obviously the administrative part of the firm. The window of a ground floor office opens and Stan calls out of it.

STAN. Ray! Ray!

Raymond goes over.

STAN. It all went off then did it?

RAYMOND. Yes. He didn't seem as hostile as the others.

STAN. Hostile? You didn't tell me anything about hostile.

RAYMOND. No, I didn't mean hostile. I mean he was more like just an ordinary bloke.

STAN. Oh. So there's no problems for me then? Because I'm empowered to use the telephone in this office any time I want to, you know that.

RAYMOND. No, it's all right Stan. See you.

STAN. Well cheer up. Behold the conquering hero comes – all that.

RAYMOND. Yes.

Raymond walks on.

STAN (*over his shoulder*). All right Mrs Carter! Windows are made for opening you know!

He closes the window.

15. Interior. Supply department. Day.

Rack upon rack stacked with electrical components, some boxed and some loose. It is the job of the work force there to fill orders sent to them from the assembly department. They walk about with clipboards finding – or not finding – the required components. When an order is filled it is sent 'upstairs' by means of a dumb waiter type of lift. Four men are at work: Terry who, God help him, has a joke for every occasion – Old Spud who has seen better days but doesn't remember them very accurately – Graham who is a bag of wind and Mike who is a large respector of physical prowess and little else. They all wear brown overalls. Only Spud's is clean.

TERRY. 3–1–6.

MIKE (*ad libbing with numbers*).

Graham places an order in the lift and shouts up the shaft.

GRAHAM. 417 – 2–Zero–Zero–One. 308A! I said job number 308A! (*Pause.*) You'll get 304 when we learn to read your rotten writing! (*He withdraws his head quickly.*) He's gobbed down that lift shaft again! I'll have him – I will.

MIKE. *I* would.

TERRY. Gob back up Graham. Go on – disprove the theory of gravity. (*He laughs at his own joke as he always does.*)

SPUD. People never gobbed in the thirties. They had too much respect – they'd have got sacked.

GRAHAM. I'll give him thirty thou copper wiring. They think we're made of it down here.

TERRY. Give my missus a shock if we was.

MIKE. Last time your missus had a shock was on her honeymoon.

SPUD. Now don't start getting filthy, boys.

TERRY. Look Spud, just because yours hasn't had an airing since Mafeking night . . .

SPUD. I'm not answering that.

TERRY. 'Course you're not. Here Graham, I bet every time he takes his pants off, a whole swarm of moths fly out.

GRAHAM. No, I'm just saying. If he gobs down that shaft once more, I'm waiting for him in the car park.

MIKE. What are you going to do? Beep your hooter and make him jump?

SPUD. All right lads – come on now – knuckle down, knuckle down. We've got those SX70's to clear up.

Nobody takes any notice. Raymond comes in. Terry sees him first.

TERRY. Aye, aye – here he is! Killer Collis! Very well done my son. Well done.

GRAHAM. Yes. Good on you Raymond.

Raymond takes off his coat and exchanges it for a brown overall, which is second in cleanliness only to Spud's.

RAYMOND. Oh. You know then?

TERRY. Yes, Stan told us. Put him in hospital eh?

GRAHAM. If I'd have come across him I'd have put him in the bloody cemetery.

MIKE. Did you go for his pressure points Ray?

RAYMOND. I don't even know what pressure points are. No, I hit him with this club thing I have on my wall.

MIKE. Clubbed him eh? Lovely, lovely. (*To Graham.*) See that? Mild old Ray – no hanging about in car parks – just upped and clubbed him. (*To Raymond.*) I respect you for that boy.

SPUD. Well I'm not a violent man Raymond, but I think burglars should be hung. We never had burglars in the thirties. You could go out of the house and leave a ten month old baby in it's basket in those days.

TERRY. Oh come off it Spud. You must have had burglars.

SPUD. No. All this burgling that's going on these days I put down to lack of values – a lack of standards of values. Nothing's been the same since they abolished the death sentence.

MIKE. No, I agree. Which is why it is down to the ordinary man – like Raymond – to protect his property and his livelihood and his station in life, that's what I think.

TERRY. Right. It's a blow for the silent majority.

GRAHAM. I'd just like to see the man who'd try anything in my house.

MIKE. Look, why don't you shut up? Somebody *has* tried it in Ray's house and he's actually done something about it.

RAYMOND. Yes, but how far can you go?

MIKE. Who?

RAYMOND. The householder. I mean, you hear expressions like . . . I don't know . . . reasonable force.

GRAHAM. Reasonable force, yes.

RAYMOND. But what is reasonable force? I mean, I hit this burglar with the first thing that came to hand. What if he dies? Is that still reasonable force?

TERRY. Of course it is.

MIKE. Give your mouth a rest and consider the question Terry. Don't just say the first thing that comes into your head. Ray, because he is the kind of bloke he is, has raised a highly moral question. What is reasonable force if you catch a burglar? Anything – that's your answer.

SPUD. They still have the birch in the Isle of Skye you know.

GRAHAM. Yes well if it had been me there wouldn't have been any question of coming to the birch because the bloke would have been splattered all up Delmont Drive.

MIKE. Look, don't keep taking the story off Ray. Make the tea, Spud.

SPUD. I'm not the boy here.

TERRY. Yes, come on Ray. Tell us all the details of what happened. Talk us through it.

RAYMOND. All right. Well I was in bed.

TERRY. With the wife I hope! No, sorry – that was a good one. I just couldn't help coming out with it. Sorry. Go on.

RAYMOND. And Sylvia woke me up. So I went out into the hall and all of a sudden the front room door opened and I thought it was a crouching figure so I grabbed my knobkerrie...

TERRY (*sniggers*). Beg your pardon, Ray.

RAYMOND. And I hit him.

MIKE. And no messing.

GRAHAM. How do you mean, you thought it was a crouching figure? If it was the bloke – which it was – it must have been him crouching.

RAYMOND (*quickly*). Oh yes – yes. And now he's in hospital.

GRAHAM. So?

RAYMOND. Well what if he dies?

SPUD. Things like that didn't even used to be thought about in the thirties. Serve him right if he does die.

RAYMOND. Oh come on Spud.

MIKE. No, that is not your responsibility – it's his for going out thieving in the first place. And if he does – and I tell you frankly Ray, your standing has gone up a lot in my eyes – there are four of us here who will be witnesses for you.

RAYMOND. You didn't see anything.

MIKE. Character witnesses. You have stood up for all of us – all the decent people in this country.

TERRY. Yeah, I agree with all that but you don't tell it as much of a story Ray. I mean, what was the bloke like? Did he square up to you or what? It's all coming out a bit BBC2 News with you.

RAYMOND. Look, I'd really sooner not talk about it.

TERRY. Oh go on.

MIKE. Look, respect a man's personality will you Terry? Ray is a naturally quiet bloke. If he don't want to talk about it he don't want to talk about it. You have a drink with me one night Ray.

RAYMOND. Yes. Excuse me.

Raymond heads out of the supply department.

SPUD. Where are you going? The tea's made.

RAYMOND. I'm just popping out for a minute.

He goes. The others settle down with their teas.

GRAHAM. Dead retiring isn't he?

TERRY. Yeah. You'd have had a bloody tannoy fixed up by now.

SPUD. I've always thought that Ray was a bit below himself on the floor you know.

MIKE. Agreed. But at least he's not one of them intellectuals who never does nothing.

16. Interior. Works corridor. Day.

BLACK MAN (*emerging from loo*). Right on Man.

Raymond walks along the corridor. A worker from another department walks past. He ducks and guards himself as though Raymond were going to strike him, then laughs, gives Raymond the 'thumbs up' and walks on. Raymond nods and smiles but without humour. He gets to an S.T.D. telephone on the wall and looks for a number in one of the directories. As he does so, Miss Benson comes along. She is in her middle twenties and a secretary – smart and young executive fodder as opposed to shop floor fodder – except for today.

MISS BENSON (*warmly*). Good morning Mr Collis.

Ray is surprised. He did not expect her to greet him.

RAYMOND. Oh. Good morning Miss...

MISS BENSON. Benson – Jane actually. Funny isn't it, how you work in a place for ages and you never get to know everybody?

RAYMOND. Well I have seen you before but ... (*Now he finds that she is standing just that little bit too close.*)

MISS BENSON. It's all round what you did to that burglar. Exciting isn't it?

RAYMOND. No.

MISS BENSON. No, well it must have been awful for you of course. What I mean is that it's so refreshing to actually know somebody who did something about it. I mean, these days I sometimes wonder whether the sexual roles haven't got totally mixed up don't you? I mean, Women's Lib is all very well but when you come down to it, a woman still basically wants a man to be a man – well I know I do anyway.

RAYMOND. I asked you to dance at the firm's 'do' last year.

MISS BENSON. Did you? You didn't.

RAYMOND. I did.

MISS BENSON. Well I'm truly sorry. Oh no – that's right. Quite honestly Mr Collis, I should never have come last year because I was up to my eyes with worry about the flat and everything. Anyway, thank goodness Eileen's moved out now so I've got the place to myself. (*She squeezes his arm.*) Listen to me telling you my life story, with you wanting to make a phone call. Still now we've broken the ice...

She gives him one of her very best smiles and walks away, wiggling her bum. Raymond knows she has been giving him the 'come on' and shakes his head sadly at the reason. He has found the number in the book and dials. He puts the coin in.

RAYMOND. Hello? St James's? I'm enquiring about a patient – he's probably in your intensive care unit. (*Head ringing.*) I don't know his name. He was admitted with a head injury and he's very short.

17. Interior. Hall. Evening.

Raymond comes in from work. He looks a bit happier.

RAYMOND. Sylvie!

SYLVIA (*voice only*). In the kitchen!

18. Interior. Kitchen. Evening.

Sylvia is laying the table. Raymond comes in.

RAYMOND. His skull isn't fractured. He's only got concussion. They're discharging him tomorrow.

SYLVIA. I know. His name's Hackett by the way. Tiny Hackett would you believe?

RAYMOND. *How* do you know?

SYLVIA. Because the Police came round again and they told me. They also told me something much more important than that.

Raymond waits to be told. She does not carry on.

RAYMOND. Well come on. What?

SYLVIA. You're not going to be charged with anything. That Chief Inspector God Almighty or whatever he calls himself has decreed that there is no case for you to answer. (*Raymond sighs and sits down with relief.*) You'd think they wouldn't use a police car when they come to tell you something like that – stuck outside the house for all to see.

RAYMOND. What time was this then?

SYLVIA. About three o'clock.

RAYMOND. I've been sweating blood all afternoon. You could have phoned me.

SYLVIA. Oh yes. Yes I could have phoned you and let the world and his wife know our business. You know what switchboard operators are like.

RAYMOND. She's very nice, Mrs Bunting. She's blind.

SYLVIA. Doesn't mean to say her mouth doesn't work does it? (*A thought.*) And whilst we're on the subject, how come *you* know about his skull not being fractured?

RAYMOND. I phoned the hospital.

SYLVIA. Oh God Almighty Raymond!

RAYMOND. What?

SYLVIA. We agreed – this morning we agreed. Nobody else was to know anything – and the first thing you do is phone up a public hospital and give another switchboard operator your name.

RAYMOND. I didn't.

SYLVIA. You must have done. They won't give out any information unless they know who's calling.

RAYMOND. Well they made a mistake then because they gave me the information first and then they asked who I was.

SYLVIA. And you told them of course.

RAYMOND. I didn't as a matter of fact. I said I was William Huntley.

SYLVIA. Who?

RAYMOND. It was the first name that came into my head. Then I put the phone down.

SYLVIA. Well by the skin of your teeth Raymond. Now was I or was I not right? All this is going away just like I said. It'll be a nine-day wonder that's all. No mention of dwarves. No mention of you picking the wrong kind of person to hit.

RAYMOND. It's ridiculous at work. Anyone would think I was some kind of hero.

SYLVIA. Well I'm sure you can stand that. Now was I right or was I wrong?

RAYMOND. Well I suppose you were right.

SYLVIA. Thank you.

RAYMOND. It's just that somewhere in all this mix-up ... I've just got a feeling that I've got some rights too.

The door chimes go. Raymond goes to answer.

19. Interior. Hall. Evening.

As Raymond goes to open the door, Sylvia watches from the kitchen. Raymond opens the door. The caller is a reporter.

REPORTER. Good evening. Mr Raymond Collis?

RAYMOND. That's right.

REPORTER. Do you think I could come in for a few minutes? We understand that it was you who had the set-to with Mr Hackett last night?

RAYMOND. No!

REPORTER. We have checked the facts.

RAYMOND. Well yes but...

Sylvia is quickly up the hall.

SYLVIA. Just a minute. Who are you?

REPORTER. Sorry. Didn't I say? Press.

SYLVIA. No. Get out. Go on.

REPORTER. We want a balanced article Mrs Collis – it is Mrs Collis isn't it? So if we could just get your side of it...

SYLVIA. We've got nothing to say. Nothing! Now clear off! (*Sylvia slams the door in his face and rounds on Raymond.*) Well?

RAYMOND. Oh God, it's going to be in the papers.

SYLVIA. And how did it get in the papers? You've let it out haven't you?

RAYMOND. No!

SYLVIA. Somebody has.

RAYMOND. Obviously.

SYLVIA. So just tell me this. What am I going to do now?

RAYMOND. *You?*

20. Exterior. A road. Day.

Norman Tuck comes out of a newsagents with Prince and a morning paper. He stops and searches the paper, then finds what he wants. He doesn't read the article but looks at it's size.

TUCK. We're in Prince. We're in. Look at that. Three inch double column – upper and lower case Bold headline. *And* we're on the same page as the air tragedy.

21. Interior. Kitchen. Day.

Raymond is making his own sandwiches. Sylvia is pouring Stan a cup of tea. Stan is tapping the newspaper he is holding and looking martyred.

STAN. Why didn't you tell me? Why didn't you tell me? You see, there was a ramification that came up. There was the dwarf. And I didn't know about it.

RAYMOND. Well with the greatest respect Stan, say you had known it was a dwarf? What difference would it have made?

STAN. I would have thought that was self-evident. Steps.

RAYMOND. How do you mean – 'Steps?'

STAN (*tapping the paper*). This! This! It's very possible that I could have stopped it ever getting into the papers.

RAYMOND. I don't see how. We don't even know how they found out about it.

STAN. No, you're missing the point Ray. There are things like injunctions for contingencies like this.

RAYMOND. Against whom?

STAN. Don't get me wrong. I'm not saying I'm a legal expert. But I will say this. I am experienced enough in life to know the value of the Mr Ridleys of this world.

RAYMOND. All right Stan, I know he was very good over the crazy paving but is he capable of slapping injunctions on newspaper editors – particularly when they've only printed the truth?

STAN. I don't know but we could have tried him and, failing him – had you told me – who knows, I could have taken it to the Ombudsman – you see, there's another outlet. But I never got a chance to try it did I?

RAYMOND. I'm sorry Stan. If there's anybody we'd have told it would have been you.

STAN. But you didn't.

RAYMOND (*feeling wretched*). No.

STAN. Well I can't say anything to that Ray because that is your judgement and I have to respect it. But to me you see, friendship – real friendship – and I hope I'm not imposing myself when I say I am this family's best friend . . .

RAYMOND. Oh you are.

STAN. Thank you for that. You see to me real friendship means total honesty. I give it and if I don't get it back and I respect your right not to think the same way as me – then I get hurt. Perhaps it's because I'm a quarter Welsh, I don't know, but hurt is what I feel.

Raymond feels he has to apologise.

RAYMOND. I'm sorry Stan but as it wasn't a normal-sized burglar – well you know what people are – we just thought we'd keep it to ourselves that's all. Sylvie and I discussed it and that was our decision.

SYLVIA. And I should never have (*rises*) allowed you to over-rule me on it.

RAYMOND. What?

SYLVIA. I wanted to tell you Stan. I wanted to tell the truth from the very beginning.

Raymond is shocked.

RAYMOND. You bloody liar!

22. Exterior. A road. Day.

Stan is driving Raymond to work. Raymond is very upset and keeps shaking his head.

RAYMOND. It's incredible. She just stood in that kitchen and lied. She dumped me.

STAN. She was upset Ray.

RAYMOND. No. I know things haven't been over-bright with Sylvie and me for a long time but that!

STAN. Ray, listen to me. This is Stan speaking now. You know I love you both.

RAYMOND. Oh I'm not asking you to take sides Stan. Christ, I was feeble enough to go along with not telling the whole story from the off. I realise it makes me come out as some sort of bloody fool, but I just thought Sylvie would stick by me that's all.

STAN. It's stand up and be counted isn't it?

RAYMOND. What is?

STAN. Time – for me. I've said I love you both and I do, but I know in my heart of hearts Ray that what Sylvia did was wrong. Very wrong.

Stan pulls up in the factory yard.

RAYMOND. I don't know if I can forgive her Stan.

STAN. No, no Ray. Time is a great healer. You must hang onto your marriage at all costs.

RAYMOND. That's what I've always thought but ... Oh I'm sorry Stan. I shouldn't be off-loading all this onto you.

Raymond gets out of the car and starts across the yard. Stan slides to the open window.

STAN. Ray!

Raymond stops.

STAN. You off-load as much as you want boy. There's a lot of untrustworthy people in this world. I'm not bumming my load but I'm not one of them..

Raymond is touched.

RAYMOND. Thanks Stan. Thanks a lot.

Raymond walks off.

23. Interior. Office corridor. Day.

We go with Raymond. Miss Benson is crossing the corridor from one office to another.

RAYMOND. Good morning Miss Benson.

Miss Benson walks past, ignoring him totally.

24. Interior. Supply department. Day.

Raymond comes in. Nobody else is in sight. Raymond assumes the others are behind the shelves somewhere.

RAYMOND. 'Morning lads!

TERRY (*sound only*). Give us a hand Ray would you?

Raymond follows the sound of the voice.

RAYMOND. Yes. What's up?

He is confronted by Terry – kneeling.

TERRY. I can't reach this shelf.

Graham looks on like a giggling child. He and Terry laugh. Raymond instantly knows that they know.

RAYMOND. Well why don't you try standing up?

GRAHAM. He's right Terry. With your head at that level you're likely to get clumped with a knobkerrie.

RAYMOND (*crossly*). I see.

Raymond turns and goes to put his brown coat on. He does not notice that there is a broad yellow stripe painted down the back of it. Terry comes back round the corner of the rack – still on his knees.

TERRY (*singing*).
Four foot two, eyes of blue, Hackett met his Waterloo.
Has anybody seen my dwarf?

He and Graham laugh again.

RAYMOND. That's really subtle that is Terry.

TERRY. Yes. About as subtle as a thump on the head with a knobkerrie.

Terry gets up – laughing.

GRAHAM. We read the paper you know Raymond.

RAYMOND. Yes. I'd sort of worked that out.

Mike appears from behind a rack. He puts a tray of components in the dumb waiter.

MIKE. One or two gaps in yesterday's version wasn't there Raymond?

RAYMOND. All right. I should have said he was a dwarf.

MIKE (*off*). Well why bloody didn't you?!

GRAHAM. No, he just let us stand here and make bloody fools of ourselves didn't he?

RAYMOND. I didn't want to talk about it at all.

MIKE. Of course you didn't. Hello Spud.

Spud comes in carrying the newspaper. He waves it at Raymond.

SPUD. We used to have respect for midgets in the thirties.

RAYMOND. Dwarf! So long as we're going to talk about it all day, the word is 'dwarf'.

SPUD. Same thing.

RAYMOND. It isn't!

GRAHAM. Oh don't split hairs. Just because you hit one, doesn't make you an expert.

MIKE. Exactly. They're still little blokes aren't they? What was you saying Spud?

SPUD. The old Queen Mary built a home for them out of her own pocket.

GRAHAM. That's right – that's right – she did.

RAYMOND. Where?

GRAHAM. Spud?

SPUD. I don't know where – but there was one. It was just about the time the Seamen's Missions were coming into being – all round about then. She did a lot of things like that, the old Queen Mary.

RAYMOND. Your brain's going.

MIKE. Oy! Oy! That'll be enough of that and all. We know you haven't got any respect for dwarves, but have a bit of respect for age!

RAYMOND. That's rich, coming from you. You called him a 'senile old git' the other day.

MIKE. I'm warning you Ray – I'm warning you!

SPUD. Nowadays, anybody with a bit of a drawback – he's at the mercy of society isn't he?

RAYMOND. I'm society!

SPUD. Exactly. Which proves my point!

RAYMOND. You wanted to hang him yesterday.

SPUD. He was normal size yesterday.

RAYMOND. Oh!

Raymond walks away.

TERRY (*reading – the newspaper*). I see Mr Raymond Collis is not available for comment again.

GRAHAM. 'Course he ain't. He ain't got a leg to stand on that's why.

SPUD. Took us all for fools.

TERRY. I thought I'd finally met Batman yesterday.

MIKE. Which was the impression he give us – yes.

GRAHAM. I can't stand people setting themselves up as things.

Raymond turns back to the others.

RAYMOND. I didn't set myself up as anything. I just told you what happened.

SPUD. Leaving out the midget bit – and I *will* maintain my right to use that word.

RAYMOND. All right, yes – but you were the ones who talked about 'a blow for decent people', and 'a man has a right to defend his own property'.

MIKE. 'Defend' is your operative word. You're not seriously telling us that you didn't know the size of the bloke you were hitting.

RAYMOND. Yes I am. I told you – I thought it was a crouching figure.

GRAHAM. Crouching figure?! You just point out to me a dwarf who looks like a crouching figure. I'll give you a hundred pounds.

Terry stoops to demonstrate.

TERRY. It doesn't hold water does it? If a dwarf, starting from here, crouches – he ends up that big – down here. To look like a normal crouching figure, it stands to reason that you have to start from a normal figure's height.

Although under stress, Raymond gets side-tracked into trying to prove a ridiculous theory.

RAYMOND. Different people have different crouches.

GRAHAM. Who?

RAYMOND. I don't know ... Rugby players.

SPUD. You never said he was a Rugby player.

RAYMOND. I'm not saying he was. I'm saying that there are degrees of crouching – but you can't just calculate them there and then if somebody suddenly comes out of a doorway.

GRAHAM. I could.

RAYMOND. How?

GRAHAM. I'd have had the light on, that's how.

RAYMOND. Well I didn't have.

GRAHAM. Oh come off it. That's the first thing anybody does if they hear noises. They put the light on.

SPUD. 'Course you had the light on.

RAYMOND. I didn't.

TERRY. I tell you one thing that doesn't ring true, my old cock – you don't seriously expect us to believe this story about this knobkerrie just happening to be hanging in your hall do you?

RAYMOND. Yes.

TERRY. Oh come on. How many halls can you point out to me that have got knobkerries hanging in them?

RAYMOND. Mine!

TERRY. Oh very convenient.

GRAHAM. No, it's as plain as a pikestaff what actually happened. You walloped him because you saw the size of him so that you could come out of it a big hero.

SPUD. In the thirties ...

RAYMOND. Oh stuff the thirties!

MIKE. See that? He's reverting to type again. He can only have goes at sixty-four year old blokes with bacon and egg of the lungs – or poor little dwarves. (*To Raymond.*) You're just like all so-called intellectuals you are – you'd never try it with somebody your own size.

RAYMOND. Look, can't you get it into your thick head? It all happened in a flash. I'd have hit him whatever his size was.

MIKE (*mockingly*). Oh – brave!

RAYMOND. No, I was terrified. I'm not a fighter. When I hit, I can't work out what exact force is required – I just hit.

MIKE. All right then (*pointing to his chin*) put one there. Go on.

RAYMOND. Why?

Mike towers over Raymond.

MIKE. So as we can see what you're like with somebody your own size.

RAYMOND. I don't want to fight you.

MIKE. 'Course you don't. I'm not Tomb Thumb am I? Go on – put one there – let's see you – go on.

Mike is prodding Raymond in the chest, driving him backwards across the shop floor. They almost collide with Mr Nesbitt who has come in unseen. Mr Nesbitt is the company chief – a self-made and self-important man.

NESBITT. What's this Wakefield?

MIKE. Nothing Mr Nesbitt, just a discussion.

NESBITT (*not believing this*). Oh yes?

He looks from one to the other. They all decide to start work.

I'd like to see you in my office Collis please.

Mr Nesbitt walks out. Raymond changes his brown coat for his jacket. As he does so he sees the yellow stripe down its back. He flings the coat angrily across the shop floor and follows Mr Nesbitt out.

25. Interior. Mr Nesbitt's office. Day.

An old-fashioned office – the holy of holies – brown wood panelling and heavy furniture. On the wall behind Mr Nesbitt's desk are self-consciously displayed two posters. One for Oxfam and one for Doctor Barnardo's. Mr Nesbitt comes in, followed by Raymond, who shuts the dor.

NESBITT. Sit down Collis.

Raymond does so. Mr Nesbitt sits, sighs heavily and looks martyred.

Well, what can I say?

RAYMOND. What about?

NESBITT. I think you know. As a matter of fact, I was rather hoping that you'd have come to see me of your own accord – at least to prepare me.

RAYMOND. I'm sorry Mr Nesbitt – prepare you for what?

NESBITT (*as if it were self-explanatory.* Raymond – I am going to the Electrical Components Exhibition this afternoon.

RAYMOND. Yes?

NESBITT. And who am I going to meet there? Our competitors in the trade.

RAYMOND. Yes.

NESBITT. Well say my secretary hadn't shown me this. (*He opens a drawer, takes out the newspaper and lays it on the desk with quiet dramatic emphasis.*) Where would I have stood then Raymond?

RAYMOND. But that happened in my house. How does it affect the Company?

NESBITT. All right – step by step if you must have it that way. What is Mrs Bunting our telephonist?

RAYMOND. She's a blind lady.

NESBITT. Uh-huh. Tommy the doorman?

RAYMOND. Well he's only got one arm, but I don't see . . .

NESBITT. Let me finish please Raymond. Give me the names of the two tea-ladies.

RAYMOND. Mrs Ho Li and Mrs Uddin.

NESBITT. From Hong Kong and Bangladesh respectively. Now what do these people have in common?

RAYMOND. Um … I think you're going to have to tell me Mr Nesbitt.

NESBITT. Yes I'm afraid I am. They are all Unfortunates. Now I don't know whether you realise this, but it has always been my philosophy with this company to take my full quota of Unfortunates. I don't have to. I haven't put myself under the umbrella of Government training schemes – I prefer to do it privately.

RAYMOND. Well I think that's very good Mr Nesbitt, I really do. But I don't see what it's got to do with me.

NESBITT. No. What was that man you struck in your house?

RAYMOND. A dwarf.

NESBITT (*correcting Raymond*). An Unfortunate.

Mr Nesbitt leans back as though resting his case.

RAYMOND. Oh I see. I'm a bad advertisement for you.

NESBITT. I'll go further. You have torpedoed my credibility.

RAYMOND. Why? It's nothing to do with you.

NESBITT. I'm afraid it is. If only every man Jack of my employees could see my policy for what it is, N.P. Components could become a moral force. What we're talking about Raymond is adverse publicity.

RAYMOND. Well I'm sorry. Next time I'm burgled I'll make sure the burglar is not an Unfortunate before I do anything about it.

NESBITT. I wish you had made sure this time. You must have noticed the size of the man.

RAYMOND. I'm just about getting fed up with this. Everybody has been telling me what I must have seen – what I must have done –

what I should have done. I did what I did *Mr* Nesbitt – it was a reflex action – that is all.

NESBITT. Against an Unfortunate.

RAYMOND (*losing his rag*). Well that's my sport isn't it? Everyone else goes to football or the dogs on Saturdays. I go around looking for dwarves to beat up. As a matter of fact *Mr* Nesbitt, I've been meaning to suggest to you that we start a dwarf-bullying society here at the Company. Or perhaps I should go to the Sports Section about it.

Mr Nesbitt looks more martyred than ever.

NESBITT. I hardly think that flippancy is called for.

RAYMOND. Maybe not. I'm just fed up with being the villain of the piece. I was the one that was broken into, and nobody seems to think that I've got any rights.

NESBITT. Surely Raymond, we that are whole have a responsibility.

RAYMOND. For what?

NESBITT. Unfortunates!

RAYMOND. Oh blimey!

NESBITT. Very well. I don't seem to be getting through to you, so I don't think there's any point in continuing this conversation.

Raymond stands up – perturbed.

RAYMOND. Mr Nesbitt – are you giving me the sack?

NESBITT. I'm not saying I'm giving you the sack Raymond, and then again I'm not saying I'm not giving you the sack. I'm saying that I have a great deal of soul-searching to do, and I hope that my decision – when it comes – will at least be humane.

RAYMOND. You are the injured party then.

NESBITT. Well at least you see that.

Mr Nesbitt assumes the pose of one wrestling with his conscience. One can almost see the stigmata on Nesbitt's palms. Raymond goes – looking punchdrunk.

26. Interior. Works offices corridor. Day.

Raymond walks back towards the supply department – dazed. Mr Samson from accounts is waiting for Raymond in a half-open doorway. He is Mr Ordinary.

SAMSON. It's Mr Collis isn't it?

RAYMOND. Yes.

SAMSON. Samson – Accounts.

RAYMOND. Oh yes.

SAMSON. I know this is neither the time nor place but I have heard about you sticking up for yourself.

RAYMOND (*pissed off*). Oh.

SAMSON. As I said, it's neither the time nor place. I'll just say this. (*He hands Raymond a leaflet with a prominent Union Jack on it.*) We are very choosy about our membership. Do try to get along.

Mr Samson goes back into his office. Puzzled, Raymond looks at the leaflet and is disgusted that anyone should think him national front material. He screws up the leaflet and throws it away, but it depresses him that bit more.

27. Interior. Court building. Day.

Stan and Raymond come in from the street.

RAYMOND. I wonder where I have to go.

STAN. My province Ray. I've been in court myself remember – over that tropical fish business. (*He goes up to a uniformed attendant.*) Good morning. Crown versus Tiny Hackett. I've got a witness here for you.

ATTENDANT. I know what you mean sir. Could I have the name please?

STAN. This is Mr Collis – Raymond Collis.

RAYMOND. That's right.

The attendant looks him up on his clipboard.

ATTENDANT. Oh yes. (*Indicating a waiting area.*) Would you sit over there please Mr Collis. You'll be called when you're wanted.

RAYMOND. Thank you.

The attendant moves away.

STAN. Right, that's got you settled in. Now listen to me Ray – this is your old Stan. Remember one thing. You are not on trial here. Your burglar is.

RAYMOND. I'm glad you reminded me Stan. The way everybody's been going on these past few days, I was beginning to wonder.

STAN. Not your old Stan.

RAYMOND. No not you. Thanks for everything. Thanks for the lift – you know.

STAN. No words Ray – no words needed. I'd stay to keep you company but I think it's probably best that I go back to your place and have a word with Sylvia.

RAYMOND. You'd have thought she'd have come with me, wouldn't you?

STAN. Yes you would. And I think it's about time she realised what *you're* going through. In the meantime, you concentrate on this afternoon because you're on your last lap now.

RAYMOND. God I hope so!

STAN. You are – while I – and I'll put it bluntly Ray, I'm going to see Sylvia now and I'm going to have a right go at her.

RAYMOND (*hopeless*). Nothing's too much trouble for you is it mate?

STAN. Can't help myself boy. It's the way I'm made.

Stan backs away making reassuring gestures, then goes. Raymond goes to sit down in the waiting area that was indicated by the attendant. Almost opposite him sits Mrs Hackett, Tiny's mother. She is obviously not very well off and has the look of someone worn out by a life of tribulation.

MRS HACKETT (*tired, without aggro*). So – you're this Mr Collis are you?

RAYMOND. How do *you* know me?

MRS HACKETT. I heard the man say.

RAYMOND. Oh.

MRS HACKETT. I'm Tiny's mother.

This is the last person in the world that Raymond wants to meet.

RAYMOND. Oh. How do you do Mrs Hackett. Do we shake hands or what?

MRS HACKETT. If you like.

RAYMOND. How do you do?

They shake hands horribly formally. Raymond sits down again. There is a silence. Raymond looks round, wanting desperately to be called. He is not. He nods towards the double doors leading into the court.

Have they started yet?

MRS HACKETT. I don't know. There's so many cases you see. I'm just waiting here with his mac.

RAYMOND. How's his head?

MRS HACKETT. Doctor said judging by his pupils it's getting back to normal, but there's a nasty big bruise under his hair.

RAYMOND. I wouldn't wilfully fracture anybody's skull you know.

MRS HACKETT. Well you didn't did you?

RAYMOND. No, but I could have.

MRS HACKETT. Everybody keeps saying knobkerrie. What's one of those?

RAYMOND (*awkwardly*). It's a Zulu war club.

MRS HACKETT. Ooh!

She holds her own head imagining what it would feel like.

RAYMOND. It was a present.

MRS HACKETT. Funny present.

RAYMOND. Yes. (*Pause. Raymond feels he has got to explain.*) Mrs Hackett?

MRS HACKETT. Yes?

RAYMOND. Look, I don't know what you've been told, but when it happened – I want you to believe me – I just sort of lashed out in the dark.

MRS HACKETT. Spur of the moment sort of thing.

RAYMOND. Yes. Only some people have got it firmly into their heads that when I saw your son was . . . small . . .

MRS HACKETT. A dwarf.

RAYMOND. A dwarf – *then* I decided to hit him. I didn't *decide* anything.

MRS HACKETT. I can see that.

RAYMOND. Can you?

MRS HACKETT. Yes. You don't have the look of the sort of person who would chuck his weight about. People do – people have – but you don't have that set about you. I can tell by your shoes and everything.

Raymond does not understand the equation but is pleased that it has been made.

RAYMOND. Thank you very much Mrs Hackett.

MRS HACKETT (*reproachfully*). Only I wish you had looked first.

RAYMOND. So do I.

MRS HACKETT. This is his first offence you know.

RAYMOND. Oh good. No, I mean . . .

MRS HACKETT. But if I'm honest with myself I could have virtually predicted that something like this was in the offing. He's been so moody.

RAYMOND (*not really wanting to know*). Has he?

MRS HACKETT. I think it was the Pantomime that really got him down. He was up for it you see – in Bromley. He's with this Agency in Greek Street – not full-time but they have got him bits and pieces in the past . . . Well, at Bromley, he was in the last eight as one of the Seven Dwarves – Snow White – you know.

RAYMOND. Oh, he's an actor?

MRS HACKETT. No. Not really. They just put him in because he would look authentic as a dwarf – I mean you must have dwarves to play the Seven Dwarves. I have seen it done with kiddies, but I never think it looks very convincing do you?

RAYMOND. No . . . no. Which one was he?

MRS HACKETT. Well, none of them in the end. He was the one of the eight who wasn't chosen. I did have hopes that he would have got Grumpy but they already had one who knew all the lines and everything. So it came down in the end – because I went up with him – that it was between him and this other man as to who played Happy. Well, one look at this other man and you could see that he'd get it. Because he has a most winning sort of personality on him – and a very good tumbler to boot. Whereas my Tiny, with the best will in the world, hasn't got any acting talent. Anyway, we come out of the Theatre and we had a cup of tea. That's when it started – his mood. Tiny said to me, 'Mum,' he said, 'I can't even get a job as a dwarf.'

RAYMOND. What does Mr Hackett think about things now that Tiny's got himself into trouble?

MRS HACKETT. Oh there's no Mr Hackett. He went back to the Merchant a week after Tiny was born. No, it's just Tiny and me – always will be I dare say.

RAYMOND. You never know. He might get married. Might meet someone like himself.

MRS HACKETT. That's what people don't understand you see. Just because you're a dwarf, don't mean to say you want to marry one. We did think once – Beryl her name was – pretty girl – normal sized – I mean they got on ever so well together. She'd out-stare anyone she would. But . . . nothing came of it in the end. Oh I know what you're thinking. You're thinking what everybody thought – geese don't marry ducks. But it was nothing to do with physical. She just went off him as a man. You know – personality. She cried and cried when she told me, but I believed her and I don't care what anybody says.

RAYMOND. Because you knew you were right.

MRS HACKETT. Yes.

RAYMOND. Well that's the trouble with feeling right.

MRS HACKETT. How do you mean?

RAYMOND. In my case I feel I'm right – at the very root of it I feel I'm right – but I can't exactly explain why. This may come out as sounding really callous to you Mrs Hackett, but I feel I was right to hit your son.

An usher comes out of the courtroom doors.

USHER. Mr Collis?

RAYMOND. Oh. Yes. (*He gets up. To Mrs Hackett.*) Do you see what I mean?

MRS HACKETT. You'd better go in.

Raymond goes into the courtroom.

28. Interior. Court building. Day.

Mix away and back to same scene. The doors of the courtroom are open and disgorge the occupants. Strangely Mr Nesbitt is with Mrs Hackett and Tiny. They move towards the street doors, talking earnestly, Mrs Hackett and Tiny are obviously very grateful to Mr Nesbitt. Raymond comes out towards the back of the crowd and sees Mr Nesbitt. Raymond looks very perturbed.

RAYMOND. *Mr* Nesbitt?!

Raymond makes his way towards Mr Nesbitt through the crowd. As he does so, Mrs Hackett and Tiny shake hands and go. Mr Nesbitt turns.

NESBITT. Ah Raymond. Very good verdict I thought, didn't you? First offence – probation – just about the right weight.

RAYMOND (*tight-lipped*). I'm glad he only got probation. I didn't want to hound him into prison.

NESBITT. Then why the edge in the voice? You're leaving something unsaid.

RAYMOND. All right, I'll say it. I didn't expect you to turn up here for the Defence. You didn't tell me.

NESBITT. I said that this was going to end as a moral issue.

RAYMOND. I know, but to stand up in Court and offer Tiny Hackett a job . . .

NESBITT. Well surely you don't want the poor fellow to be thrown on the midden of society.

RAYMOND. No, of course not.

NESBITT. Then how can you attack what is only a philanthropic act on my part?

RAYMOND. Because the job you're giving him is in the same shop as me. I'm going to walk in Monday morning and come face to face with him.

NESBITT. Yes?

RAYMOND. Well, it's not just 'Yes?', is it?

NESBITT. Then what is it?

RAYMOND. Embarrassment.

NESBITT. Now look Raymond – we're not children. It took me a great deal of time to come to this judgement. And if I say so myself Raymond, I think what we have here is a solution which is imbued with the philosophy of the Company – which I tried to explain to you the other day. On the one hand I have taken no action against you – despite the considerable amount of adverse publicity you attracted – and on the other hand I hope that I have *given* hope to the Unfortunate that you attacked.

RAYMOND. But it will be an impossible situation.

NESBITT. That's for you to decide. Can't you put your ego to one side for a moment?

RAYMOND. What ego? For the past couple of weeks I haven't been allowed to have an ego!

Raymond leaves angrily. Mr Nesbitt thinks how sad it is that other people cannot be as wise as he.

29. Exterior. A street near Ray's home. Night.

Raymond comes along looking deeply depressed. He meets Norman Tuck and Prince.

TUCK. Good evening Mr Collis.

RAYMOND (*sharply*). And?!

TUCK. Nothing.

RAYMOND. You mean just 'Good evening'?

TUCK. Yes.

RAYMOND. Just 'Good evening' – well-mannered, nice and pleasant?

TUCK. Why not?

RAYMOND. You must have read the paper about my burglary. You must have heard people's opinions about me.

TUCK. I have read the paper yes, but I'm not interested in tittle-tattle.

RAYMOND. Well I just wish there were more people in the world like you Mr Tuck. I wish more people would just walk their dog and mind their own business. (*To Prince.*) New collar and lead I see.

TUCK (*quickly*). Yes, I had a bit of a windfall. Goodnight then. Come on Prince – we'll go round a different way tonight.

30. Interior. Sitting room. Night.

Stan and Sylvia are watching television. Raymond enters.

RAYMOND. Hello Sylvia – Stan.

STAN. There he is!

Sylvia turns off the television set.

SYLVIA. So you condescended to come home then?

Raymond sits down.

RAYMOND. I fancied a drink, so I had one.

STAN. His Master's Voice!

Stan laughs. Sylvia does not.

SYLVIA. Well . . . are you going to bother to tell me what happened?

RAYMOND. If you'd have bothered to come you'd have found out for yourself.

STAN (*the peacemaker*). Now come on you two, come on.

RAYMOND. All right. He was found guilty – first offence – probation.

STAN. Just about what Uncle Stan reckoned wasn't it Sylvia?

SYLVIA. So what about our name?

RAYMOND. Mud – still mud! He couldn't even pass sentence without pontificating. 'Whilst on the one hand – blah, blah, blah – can't help but regret that the householder did not have the common sense to first ascertain the size of the intruder.'

STAN. I'm of the opinion that judges and magistrates should be severely curtailed.

RAYMOND. And then the goat's dropping on top of the cake, I came out of the Court to find that Nesbitt has given Tiny Hackett a job – in my department!

SYLVIA. You'll have to leave.

RAYMOND. Oh he wants me to don't worry. What would suit him is a firm full of Unfortunates so that he could crow about them! God knows what it's going to be like on Monday. I wouldn't be surprised if they don't build a grandstand for people to come and watch me squirm.

SYLVIA. You, you, you!

RAYMOND. What do you mean?

SYLVIA. You haven't given a thought to me in all this. What about when I go to Sainsbury's on Tuesday? What am I going to have to put up with?

RAYMOND. Well you copped out of your first story quickly enough. I'd be very surprised if you hadn't concocted another one to cover yourself.

STAN. Now come on children – it's over – it's over.

SYLVIA. What if I have? It's your fault if I have to go round telling lies.

RAYMOND. Then tell the truth! I haven't actually done anything wrong!

SYLVIA. Then how come nobody believes you? How come everybody's treating you like dirt?

RAYMOND. Because it's a wonderful opportunity for them to prove how holier than thou they are. But I can't make them see.

SYLVIA. See what?

RAYMOND. Um . . .

SYLVIA (*loosing patience*). Oh you're useless!

STAN. No Sylvie – no, no, no. Bring me in on this Ray. See what?

Raymond trying desperately to define.

RAYMOND. Look, I've been on the receiving end since I – *I* was burgled. *I'm* the one that's being condemned. And there's a reason why I shouldn't be and I can't define it.

STAN. Well put Ray.

SYLVIA. He hasn't put anything. (*To Raymond.*) If you choose to half-kill a dwarf, don't expect anybody to be pleased with you.

RAYMOND. You were there. I didn't choose!

SYLVIA. Well I'm not even sure about that now.

RAYMOND (*cannot believe it*). What?

SYLVIA. I'm not sure you didn't see that Hackett's height and just take the opportunity to show what a big man you were. Well you're not and you never have been.

STAN. Look, we're all tired. Why don't we...

SYLVIA. Shut up! I've been married to you for fourteen years and you've never been the man in things. Nothing ever gets done unless somebody else does it for you.

RAYMOND. Like what?!

SYLVIA. Everything! Making sure the bills are paid, holidays, house maintenance. You wouldn't even go round to those people about the dog barking all night long would you?

RAYMOND. You should have married the Citizens Advice Bureau if that's what you think a man is.

SYLVIA. I don't. I know what a man is first and foremost – and you're not that either! Somebody else has to do that for you and all!

This is a terrible revelation to Raymond.

RAYMOND (*stunned*). Jesus!

Stan looks terribly guilty. He stands up.

STAN. Look, May is all by herself. I'd better...

It suddenly hits Raymond. He rounds on Stan.

RAYMOND. You bastard!

STAN. Look Ray, we're all friends here...

RAYMOND. Yes, you love us both don't you? Not much you don't!

Raymond stands up and advances on Stan who backs away. Sylvia watches – silly cow being fought over.

STAN. I'm not proud of myself Ray – don't think that.

RAYMOND. Stan the Rock – lean on me. I'll lean on you!

Raymond is ready to hit Stan. Stan immediately sits down, feigning pain in the chest.

STAN. Oh! Oh! You know I've got angina.

RAYMOND. Good!

Raymond grabs Stan by the shirt, trying to pull him to his feet so that he can knock him down.

STAN. No – Ray – no! You can't hit a man with angina Ray.

RAYMOND. I couldn't give a fart about your angina! You've been knocking off my wife.

STAN. Oh ... the pain. I think it's going through to the heart. I think I'm going to have a heart attack!

Stan cowers and strangely Raymond lets him go. Stan sinks back in the chair trying to display the signs of an imminent heart attack.

RAYMOND (*to himself*). That's it. (*To Stan.*) You aren't a bloke with angina. You're an adulterer.

STAN. I can't breathe! I can't breathe!

RAYMOND. And Tiny Hackett was not a dwarf in my house – he was a burglar.

STAN. I'm blacking out.

SYLVIA. Coward. Hit him Ray.

But Raymond – for the first time since the burglary – knows his own mind. He looks from Sylvia to Stan and back to Sylvia.

RAYMOND. No. *You* hit him.

Raymond walks out. Sylvia is dumbfounded and Stan is so surprised that he sits up, forgetting his heart attack.

31. Exterior. Works. Day.

Raymond walks in through the gates. He arrives at the window to Stan's office and stops. He taps on the window. It is opened by Mrs Carter.

RAYMOND. He won't be in today Mrs Carter – he's having a long heart attack.

Raymond moves on and into the office building.

32. Interior. Miss Benson's office corridor. Day.

Raymond and Miss Benson approach each other from opposite directions along the corridor. He can see her preparing herself to be haughty as she passes him. Raymond gets in first by tossing his head exaggeratedly.

RAYMOND. Huh!

This takes the wind out of Miss Benson's sails. Raymond smiles to himself as he walks on.

33. Interior. Mr Nesbitt's office. Day.

Mr Nesbitt is dictating.

MR NESBITT. . . . And furthermore, I must protest at your cynical insinuation that I employ the Unfortunates of our society as a means of reducing my wage bill. Stop. My brand of Christianity dictates that. (*A knock at the door.*) Come in. (*Raymond comes in. Nesbitt is taken aback.*) Collis!

RAYMOND. Yes. Good morning Mr Nesbitt. Just thought you'd like to know that I have turned up.

MR NESBITT (*on the defence*). Ah. And very delighted I am to see you.

RAYMOND. I thought you would be Mr Nesbitt.

MR NESBITT. Indeed. I'll go further. I can't think of a better way to start the week than to think that something I may have said to you has given you a grasp of what I consider is a very important philosophy.

RAYMOND. It's all right, I don't need it. I've got one of my own. That's why I turned up.

Raymond goes. Mr Nesbitt smiles but then has a feeling that he has been got at. This is reinforced when he sees his secretary suppressing a laugh.

34. Interior. Supply department. Day.

Spud is showing Tiny Hackett the ropes.

SPUD. No, look, I'll go through it again. The job sheet is boxed and you tick off your components in your left-hand box and your quantity in your right-hand box. So, what have we got? We've got 2 dozen F.69 terminals. So it goes – tick, F.69 terminals, 2 dozen. Not – 2 doz, F.69 terminals, tick.

We move away to where Mike, Terry and Graham are gathered – gossiping.

GRAHAM. I'd turn up, I'd turn up. But we're not talking about me are we? We're talking about Ray.

MIKE. 'Course he won't turn up. He ain't got the bottle has he?

TERRY. Well I hope he does.

MIKE. Why? You on his side all of a sudden?

TERRY. No. It'll be a giggle though won't it? It'll be a question of who has a go at who first when he comes face to face with . . . er . . . what's name. (*Terry points behind his hand at Tiny. Raymond walks in. The atmosphere is tense.*) Eyes down.

RAYMOND. Good morning everybody. (*Making a point of it but neutrally.*) Good morning Mr Hackett.

TINY (*also neutral*). Good morning Mr Collis.

Raymond puts on his brown coat with the yellow stripe and starts work. The others look disappointed at the lack of fireworks.

TERRY. What a fiddle!

35. Interior. Supply department. Day. Later.

Raymond works quietly and alone. Spud is still showing Tiny Hackett the ropes – he has moved from theory to practice. Mike, Terry and Graham are working on filling the same order.

SPUD. Now, this is of paramount importance, nip out, quick.

TINY. O.K. Spud.

GRAHAM. Look – this is a proven scientific fact. Now do you want to know about it or not?

MIKE. I tell you what I want to know at the moment Graham – I want to know what they're doing upstairs with all these P.59's. I mean, what *are* they doing with them – eating them?

TERRY. It's obvious what's happening isn't it? It's Beasley. He's taking them home by the boatload.

MIKE. Why?

TERRY. Well be fair Mike – your P.59's a very nice piece of precision tooling isn't it? And I mean, if you get your furniture legs resting on P.59's it really sets your room off lovely.

GRAHAM. Look, I'm trying to talk about something sensible. In this book I read . . .

MIKE. Look shut up. So all right Terry, we've all had our P.59's away in the past, but Beasley has ordered five hundred in the last three weeks. I mean, how much furniture has he got?

GRAHAM. In this book I read . . .

MIKE. Oy, we are supposed to be working mate. (*An electric bell sounds.*) Right, tea-break. Down tools.

The 'workers' all move away from the racks and up to Mrs Holi who has entered with the tea trolley. She dishes out the tea – already poured out in paper cups. Mike, Graham and Terry are first to the trolley. They come away from it to sit in a little group. Behind them, after getting his tea, Tiny, still the new boy, goes to sit a little distance apart, as does Raymond. Spud comes to join the trio.

MIKE (*to Graham*). All right Einstein, what's this book you been reading then?

GRAHAM. Oh, I'm allowed to speak then am I?

MIKE. Shut up. Go on.

GRAHAM. Well, I have been reading this book where there is documented evidence of people simply bursting into flames for no apparent reason – spontaneous combustion.

TERRY (*singing*). 'Come on baby – light my fire.'

GRAHAM. It's true.

SPUD. One of the German Royal Family did. The old Queen Mary mentioned that in her memories.

MIKE. Shut up. Look Graham, I don't know why you come out with these ridiculous statements. O.K., here's combustion. I'll show you combustion.

But Mike cannot find the lighter.

TERRY. What just sitting there in front of the telly and bursting into flames?

MIKE. Where's me lighter? Come on. Who's got me lighter?

SPUD. What are you talking about – 'Who's got your lighter?' We ain't got your lighter.

MIKE. Well I had it when I come in. Someone's got it.

TERRY. Here Mike...

Terry scratches his head and surreptitously points towards Tiny with his thumb. They all jump to the same conclusion and stare at Tiny. Tiny becomes aware of this and looks up. They all look away. They are all convinced that Tiny has the lighter but no one has the faintest idea of what to do about it. Mike moves over to Raymond, the others following.

MIKE (*conspiratorially*). Here Ray?

RAYMOND. Yes?

MIKE. My lighter's missing.

RAYMOND. I haven't got it.

MIKE. I'm not saying you have, no. Only...

RAYMOND. Only what?

MIKE. Well...

The four nod clandestinely towards Tiny.

RAYMOND. Are you sure?

MIKE. No. Only it stands to reason with his record.

RAYMOND. What are you telling me for?

MIKE. Well ... you've had experience of dealings with him.

This is a moment for Raymond to savour.

RAYMOND. Yes. And now it's your turn.

They stand in a nonplussed group.

Tricky isn't it?

Raymond puts his feet up and goes back to his newspaper.